COOL
BOARD GAMES

CRAFTING CREATIVE TOYS & AMAZING GAMES

REBECCA
FELIX

**Checkerboard
Library**

An Imprint of Abdo Publishing
abdopublishing.com

ABDOPUBLISHING.COM

Published by Abdo Publishing, a division of ABDO, PO Box 398166, Minneapolis, Minnesota 55439. Copyright © 2016 by Abdo Consulting Group, Inc. International copyrights reserved in all countries. No part of this book may be reproduced in any form without written permission from the publisher. Checkerboard Library™ is a trademark and logo of Abdo Publishing.

Printed in the United States of America, North Mankato, Minnesota

102015
012016

THIS BOOK CONTAINS
RECYCLED MATERIALS

Content Developer: Nancy Tuminelly
Design and Production: Mighty Media, Inc.
Editor: Liz Salzmann
Photo Credits: Mighty Media, Inc., Shutterstock

The following manufacturers/names appearing in this book are trademarks:
Craft Smart®, DecoColor™, MOLOTOW™, Sharpie®

Library of Congress Cataloging-in-Publication Data
Felix, Rebecca, 1984- author.
 Cool board games : crafting creative toys & amazing games / by Rebecca Felix.
     pages cm. -- (Cool toys & games)
 Includes index.
 ISBN 978-1-68078-046-8
1. Board games--Juvenile literature. 2. Board games--Design and construction--Juvenile literature. 3. Toymakers--Juvenile literature. I. Title.
 GV1312.F45 2016
 794--dc23
                        2015033079

CONTENTS

Louisburg Library
Bringing People and Information Together

BOARD GAMES

MULTIPLE MONOPOLIES

Monopoly was first published about 80 years ago. Since then, more than 1,200 **versions** of this game have been created!

Have you ever sunk an enemy submarine in the game Battleship? Or crowned kings in checkers? Or been the banker in Monopoly? These are just a few examples of fun board games.

Board games have been around for thousands of years. In fact, archaeologists have found evidence these games existed even before recorded history! Ancient people used stone, wood, and even silver to make board games.

Today, most board games are made of cardboard and plastic. These games can have a large **variety** of themes. Some games have cards, spinners, and **intricate** pieces.

A NEW BATTLESHIP

Milton Bradley published a plastic Battleship game in 1967. Before that, people played this game using paper and pencil.

HOW BOARD GAMES ARE MADE

Think of board games you have played. Now think of all the pieces that were included in those games. In addition to a board, a game can have cards, game pieces, and tokens. And there is often a rule book too. Toy makers must make or purchase all these parts, as well as a box to keep the game in.

Developing a board game begins with an idea. A **prototype** of the idea is made and tested. Then the board game company creates many copies of the game.

Most game boards are made of a special cardboard called gray board. The gray board is cut to the correct size for the game. Then folds are made in each board. Artwork for the game is printed on industrial machines. The artwork is glued to the game boards. Then the boards are boxed with all of the game pieces and shipped to stores!

ANCIENT GAMERS

Senet is an ancient Egyptian game. Senet boards were found in King Tutankhamun's tomb. He died more than 3,000 years ago!

CHECKERS, ANYONE?

Checkers is another ancient board game. It is also called draughts (DRAHFTS).

BECOME A TOY MAKER

THINK LIKE A TOY MAKER

Board game creators come up with amazing designs. Some modern board games have lights and sounds, or even gears that move! But these features don't matter if you don't enjoy playing the game.

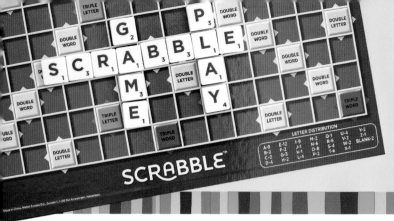

NAME GAME

Scrabble's original name was Lexico. It is from the term *lexicon*, meaning "words used in a language."

The best games are fun to play even when you don't win. And they are different each time you play them.

As you work on the projects in this book, think like a toy maker! Read the steps and look at the photos. Get inspired. Then get creative!

HAVE FUN!

Playing board games is meant to be fun. Making them should be too! Think up new twists and different ways to play the games. What features will make your game exciting? Are there special rules you want your game to have? Think of ways to make your board game **unique**. Then get to toy making!

MATERIALS

HERE ARE SOME OF THE MATERIALS YOU'LL NEED FOR THE PROJECTS IN THIS BOOK.

acrylic paint

adhesive craft foam

craft plywood

decorative stickers

dice

duct tape

foam brush

hot glue gun & glue sticks

magnetic sheet

metal tin with hinged lid

paint pens

paintbrush

10

papier-mâché box

permanent marker

plastic plates

plastic tablecloth

rolling pin

round label

round magnets

sticky note

tagboard

MINI MAGNETIC BATTLESHIP

MAKE A TINY TAKE-ALONG STRATEGY GAME OF SINKING SHIPS!

MAKE THE GAME

1 Cover your work surface with newspaper. Paint the lids of the tins. Let the paint dry.

2 Use the paint pens to color one side of each magnet. Paint eight magnets with each pen.

3 Paint a **unique** design on the remaining magnet.

(continued on next page)

MATERIALS

newspaper
2 small metal tins
 with hinged lids
acrylic paint
paintbrush
paint pens, 3 colors
25 small round
 magnets
32 small round labels
marker

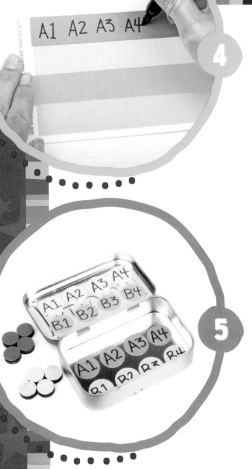

4 Make four sets of eight labels with the codes A1, A2, A3, A4, B1, B2, B3, B4.

5 Stick a set of labels inside the lid of each tin. Stick a set of labels inside the bottom of each tin.

PLAY THE GAME

1 Open both tins. Set them with their lids against each other. Use the **unique** magnet to hold them together.

2 Divide the magnets so each player has four of each color. The players decide which color will represent "hits."

3 Each player chooses a "ship" color. The players place the magnets on stickers in the bottoms of their tins.

4 Then players take turns guessing which codes their opponent's "ships" are on.

5 If a guess is correct, the other player says, "hit!" and covers the "ship" with a "hit" magnet. The guesser marks the hit by putting a magnet on that code in his or her lid.

6 If a guess is wrong, the other player says, "miss!"

7 The game ends when one player sinks all of the other player's "ships."

8 When the game is over, store the magnets inside the tins.

REFRIGERATOR WORDS

GET POINTS FOR SPELLING WORDS IN THIS VERTICAL BOARD GAME!

MAKE THE GAME

1 Use the paint pens to color one side of each large magnet.

2 Use the paint pens to write letters on the small magnets. Write each **consonant** on three magnets. Write each **vowel** on seven magnets.

3 Cover your work surface with newspaper. Paint the tagboard and the magnetic sheet. Let the paint dry.

(continued on next page)

MATERIALS

paint pens
4 large round magnets
98 small round magnets
newspaper
acrylic paint
foam brush

tagboard, 14 × 22 inches (36 × 56 cm)
magnetic sheet, 5 × 8 inches (13 × 20 cm)
ruler
pencil
scissors
sticky notes

4 Use the ruler and pencil to draw a 12-inch (30 cm) square on the tagboard. Draw lines across the square to make a **grid**. The lines should be 1 inch (2.5 cm) apart.

5 Draw a rectangle under the grid. Make it 4 by 11 inches (10 by 28 cm).

6 Trace the grid and rectangle lines with a paint pen. Let the paint dry.

7 Fold the magnetic sheet in half. Cut along the fold.

PLAY THE GAME

1 Use the large magnets to hang the game board on the refrigerator.

2 Place the letter magnets face down in the rectangle.

3 Each player gets a magnetic sheet. Then the players choose eight letters and place them on their sheets.

4 The players take turns using their letters to spell words on the game board. After each turn, players choose new letters, so they always have eight.

5 Players score one point for each letter in their words. Put a sticky note on the refrigerator to keep score on.

MEMORY GAME BOARD

DESIGN A MEMORY GAME WITH MYSTERY BOXES!

MAKE THE GAME

1 Paint the plywood and boxes. Let them dry. Decorate the box lids.

2 Space the boxes evenly on the plywood. Hot glue them in place.

PLAY THE GAME

1 When the player is not looking, put a small item inside each box.

2 The player then opens two boxes. If the items match, the player leaves the lids off.

3 If the items don't match, the player closes both boxes. The player keeps guessing until all the matches are found.

MATERIALS

craft plywood, 12 × 12 inches (30 × 30 cm)	16 papier-mâché boxes, 2½ × 2½ inches (6 × 6 cm)	acrylic paint paintbrush adhesive craft foam scissors	hot glue gun & glue sticks 8 pairs of small items that fit in the boxes

THE GAME OF YOUR LIFE

TURN YOUR LIFE EVENTS INTO A PERSONAL GAME!

MAKE THE GAME

1 Cover your work surface with newspaper. Paint the tagboard. Let the paint dry.

2 Fold the tagboard in thirds. Crease the folds. Turn the tagboard over. Fold on the same lines, creasing the folds again.

3 Draw four boxes on a piece of paper. In box 1, list fun events that have happened to you, such as, "Adopt a dog!" After each one, add a favorable game action. It could be "Take another turn."

(continued on next page)

MATERIALS

newspaper
acrylic paint
paintbrush
tagboard
paper

markers
paint pens
decorative stickers
6 to 8 items to use for game pieces
dice

1
- Hit a home run at the big game! Move forward 2 spaces.
- Get an "A" on your math test. Move forward 5 spaces.
- Adopt a dog! Take another turn.
- Learn to play the drums! Move forward 3 spaces.

4 In box 2, list fun events that could happen in the future. For example, "Get your driver's license!" They could be realistic or silly. Add a favorable action after each event.

5 In box 3, list **mishaps** that have happened to you. For example, "Get gum stuck in your hair." Add unfavorable actions after these events, such as "Move back 3 spaces."

6 In box 4, list mishaps that could happen in the future. Add an unfavorable action after each mishap.

7 Use paint pens to draw a winding path on the tagboard. Draw lines across the path to make spaces. Make sure the spaces are large enough to write in.

8 Add a "Start" space at the beginning of the path. Add a "Win" space at the end of the path.

9 Write events from your lists in the spaces on the path. Mix up the events and spread them out on the path. It's okay if some spaces are blank. Or fill them all. It's up to you!

10 Give your game a title. Decorate the game board with stickers, drawings, or designs.

(continued on next page)

PLAY THE GAME

1 The players each choose a game piece.

2 The first player rolls the dice and moves that many spaces. He or she follows the directions on the space. If the space is blank, the turn is over. Then it's the next player's turn.

3 The players keep taking turns until someone reaches the "Win" space.

THE CHECKERED GAME OF LIFE

The Game of Life is a board game created in 1860. That year, **lithographer** Milton Bradley was playing a board game with a friend. He got a great idea. He would use his lithograph printer to print a board game!

Bradley made a game board that was similar to a checkerboard. Each white square listed an event people experience in real life. Bradley called his game The Checkered Game of Life. It was a hit! The first year, more than 45,000 games were sold.

Milton Bradley Company went on to make many board games. In 1984, Hasbro purchased Milton Bradley Company. It made a modern **version** of Bradley's first board game. Today, The Game of Life is one of the best-selling games of all time!

GIANT OUTDOOR CHECKERS

CREATE A HUGE GAME BOARD TO PLAY GIANT CHECKERS OUTDOORS!

MAKE THE GAME

1 Cut the tablecloth into a square. Fold the tablecloth in half. Roll the rolling pin over the fold to make a crease.

2 Fold the tablecloth in thirds in the same direction. Crease the folds with the rolling pin.

3 Open the tablecloth. Trace over each crease using the marker and yardstick.

4 Fold the tablecloth in half the opposite way. Use the rolling pin to make a crease.

(continued on next page)

MATERIALS

rectangular plastic tablecloth	permanent marker	12 plastic plates, 6 each of two colors
rolling pin	yardstick	large mesh or plastic bag
	duct tape	

5 Fold the tablecloth in thirds in the same direction. Crease the edges each time. Open the tablecloth. Trace each new crease with the marker.

6 Cover every other square on the tablecloth with duct tape.

PLAY THE GAME

1 Spread the game board on the ground.

2 Set a plate on every other space on two rows of one side of the board. Set the other six plates on the same-colored spaces on the opposite side.

3 Follow the rules of checkers to play the game.

4 Store the board and plates in a mesh or plastic bag.

GLOSSARY

consonant – a letter of the alphabet that is not a vowel. Some of the consonants are *b*, *f*, *n*, and *r*.

grid – a pattern with rows of squares, such as a checkerboard.

intricate – having many small, related parts.

lithograph – a print made by spreading ink on a flat surface and pressing paper over it.

mini – short for miniature. A small copy or model of something.

mishap – an unfortunate accident or happening.

prototype – an original model on which something is patterned.

unique – not the same as anything else.

variety – a collection of different types of one thing. An assortment.

version – a different form or type from the original.

vowel – any of the letters *a*, *e*, *i*, *o*, and *u*.

WEBSITES

To learn more about Cool Toys & Games, visit **booklinks.abdopublishing.com**. These links are routinely monitored and updated to provide the most current information available.

INDEX